P9-CDB-583

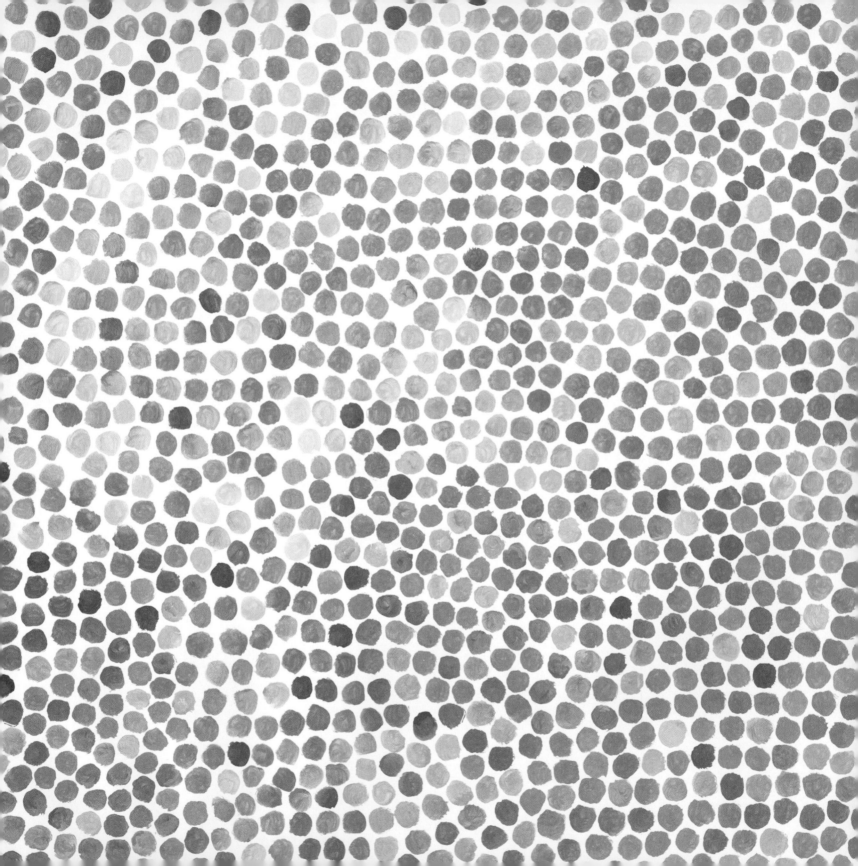

BECOMING A GOOD CREATURE

words by
SY MONTGOMERY

pictures by
REBECCA GREEN

HOUGHTON MIFFLIN HARCOURT
Boston   New York

SCHOOL IS NOT THE ONLY PLACE TO FIND A TEACHER

Sometimes we meet teachers in the forest, or in the barn, or in the ocean—or right in our own house. Some of my teachers have had two legs while others have had four or even eight. But all have taught me something important about how to be a good creature in the world.

FIND GOOD TEACHERS

But nobody could show me how—until Molly.

Molly was only a puppy when she came to live with us, but she was
already gifted with special animal powers. So I watched her. I listened.
And I learned that if we pay attention, the world outside beckons us.
Even before I started school, Molly was my first teacher.

DISCOVER YOUR PASSIONS

When I grew up, I still hungered to learn about animals.

In Australia, I met birds who stood almost as tall as I did. Emus can't fly, but they run like the wind. What were their lives like? I wanted to know.

So I moved to a tent in the wild to find out.

For many months, I followed three emus and watched them like I had watched Molly. They showed me where they traveled and what they ate. And while I followed them, they also showed me my own path: I would go to the places where animals lived. Each would be a new teacher and I would write their stories.

RESPECT
OTHERS

Next, I went to Africa to meet gorillas. I hiked in the mountains there for a long time. It was nothing like my home in New Hampshire.

As I stopped to catch my breath, I saw a person running toward me. Why? Because a big gorilla was chasing him!

But I didn't run. I crouched low and looked at the ground, as if bowing before a king. The gorilla stood, beat his chest, and let out a roar. And when he saw that I understood that he was boss, he turned and calmly led me to meet his gorilla family. Ever since that day, I've respected my animal hosts and their homes.

DON'T BE
AFRAID

In India,
I met tigers.

In Africa, lions.

In the rivers of South America,
I swam with piranhas and electric eels.

In the ocean, I met sharks.
None of them ever hurt me.

WAIT PATIENTLY

I traveled to Australia again—this time to meet a different bird. The cassowary, like the emu, is a tall bird who runs instead of flies. I was eager to meet one and spent a week trekking through their rainforest home.

No cassowary.

An hour before I had to leave, I went one more
time to say goodbye to the beautiful, empty jungle.
A cassowary stepped out from the trees before me.
He was close enough for me to see his eyelashes!
I was so glad that I had waited.

MAKE YOUR OWN FAMILY

At home, animals continued to teach me. My husband and I didn't
plan on having babies. But soon a baby came to us: a baby pig.
We named him Christopher Hogwood.

Two little girls and their mother moved in next door. They saw Chris in the backyard and came to visit every day. He was a very happy pig.

We weren't all related, but Christopher showed us that it didn't matter. We became one big family: my husband, our border collie Tess, our hens, the two little girls, and their mom. And one *very* happy pig.

SEE FOR YOURSELF

I'd heard it all before: Hyenas are ugly. Hyenas are lazy. Hyenas are thieves. They steal food from lions. Everyone said so—even *The Lion King*!

Then I visited a hyena den.

The fluffy cubs wrestled like playing puppies. Mothers tenderly licked their babies. And they weren't stealing food from lions—more often, lions stole food from *them*.

Hyenas reminded me that what everyone says is not always true.

LOVE LITTLE LIVES

I never gave spiders much thought until I met one in South America who was almost as big as a chipmunk.

She was a sleek black tarantula with toes tipped in pink, like she'd just had a fancy pedicure. She lived in a potted plant at a nature center.

We learned that she was a
gentle kind of tarantula who can live for
thirty years. We named her Clarabelle and let
her walk across our hands each night. We think
she liked us. We sure liked her. Clarabelle showed
us that little lives matter as much as big ones.

LEARN FORGIVENESS

One Christmas morning, I found an intruder in our henhouse:
a white-coated weasel.

Though tiny, weasels are fierce. They catch and eat animals
much bigger than themselves. They even eat chickens!

Towering above him, I looked into the weasel's black eyes.
Fearlessly, the little weasel stared back. How brave he was!
And how beautiful, in his snowy winter coat. I was dazzled by
his determination and couldn't be angry at his will to survive.

FIND COMMON GROUND

Octavia had eight arms, three hearts, no bones.
She lived in the water, I live on land.

We both liked to play!

As different as we were,
We became friends.

TRUST TOMORROW

The little girls next door moved away. Our pig grew old. Our dog grew old. It felt like everything was ending.

Then one day I got a phone call from our veterinarian. He told me that a neighbor's border collie had just had pups. They were all valuable dogs,

with important work to do, herding sheep, cows, and pigs when they grew up. All the babies already had farm families waiting for them. All but one—one puppy had a blind eye.

Would I take him?

Thurber taught me the best lesson of all: even in the darkest times, there may be a wonderful new teacher waiting for you, right around the corner.

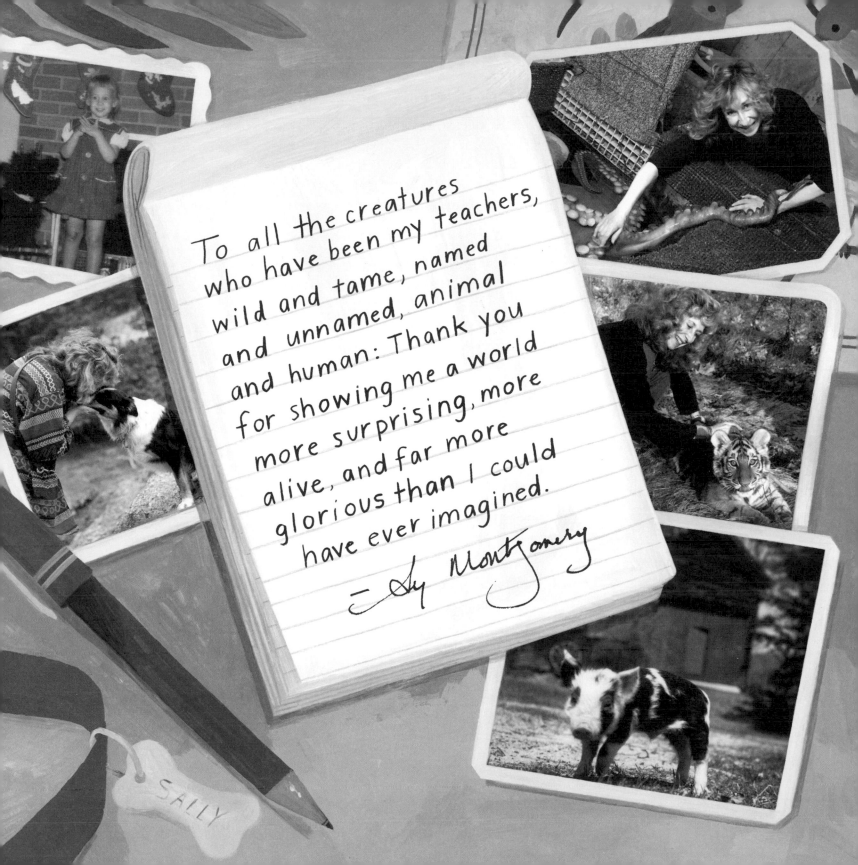

To all the creatures who have been my teachers, wild and tame, named and unnamed, animal and human: Thank you for showing me a world more surprising, more alive, and far more glorious than I could have ever imagined.

— Sy Montgomery

Always and forever, for Dr. A. B. Millmoss —S. M.

For my high school art teacher, Laura Meiers —R. G.

All rights reserved. For information about permission to reproduce selections from this book, write to trade.permissions@hmhco.com or to Permissions, Houghton Mifflin Harcourt Publishing Company, 3 Park Avenue, 19th Floor, New York, New York 10016.

hmhbooks.com

The illustrations in this book were done in Gouache on paper and edited digitally.

The text was set in Grit Primer.

Cover and interior design by Jessica Handelman

Photographs on p. 31 courtesy of the author except: Phebe Lewan (middle right) and Tianne Strombeck (bottom left).

The Library of Congress Cataloging-in-Publication data is on file.

ISBN: 978-0-358-25210-8

Manufactured in China

SCP 10 9 8 7 6 5 4 3 2 1

4500799962

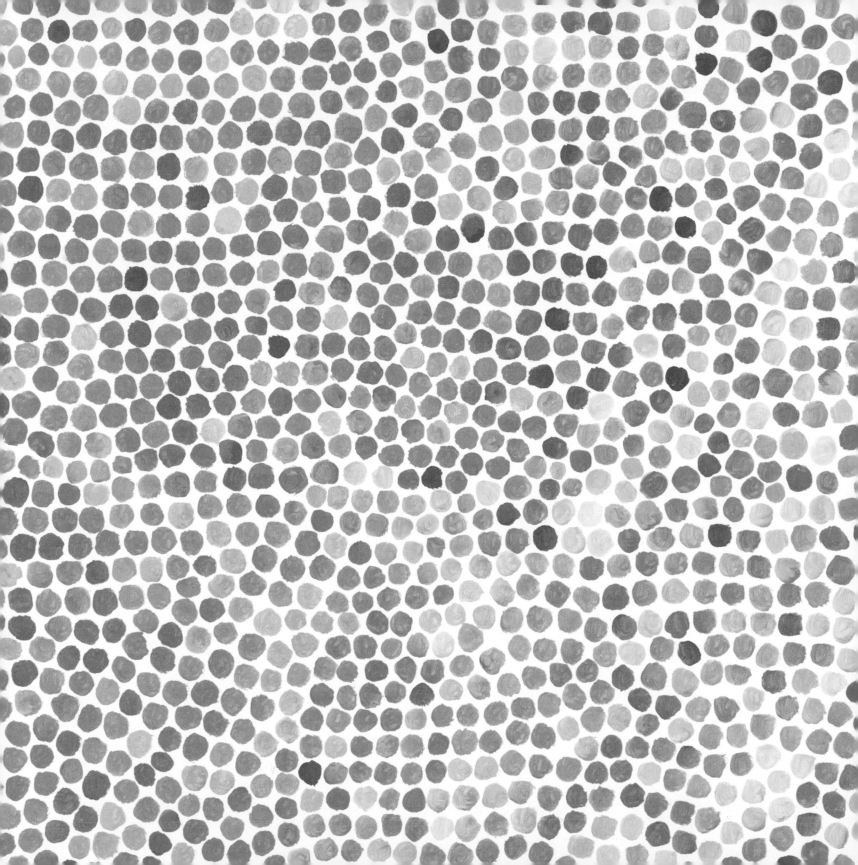

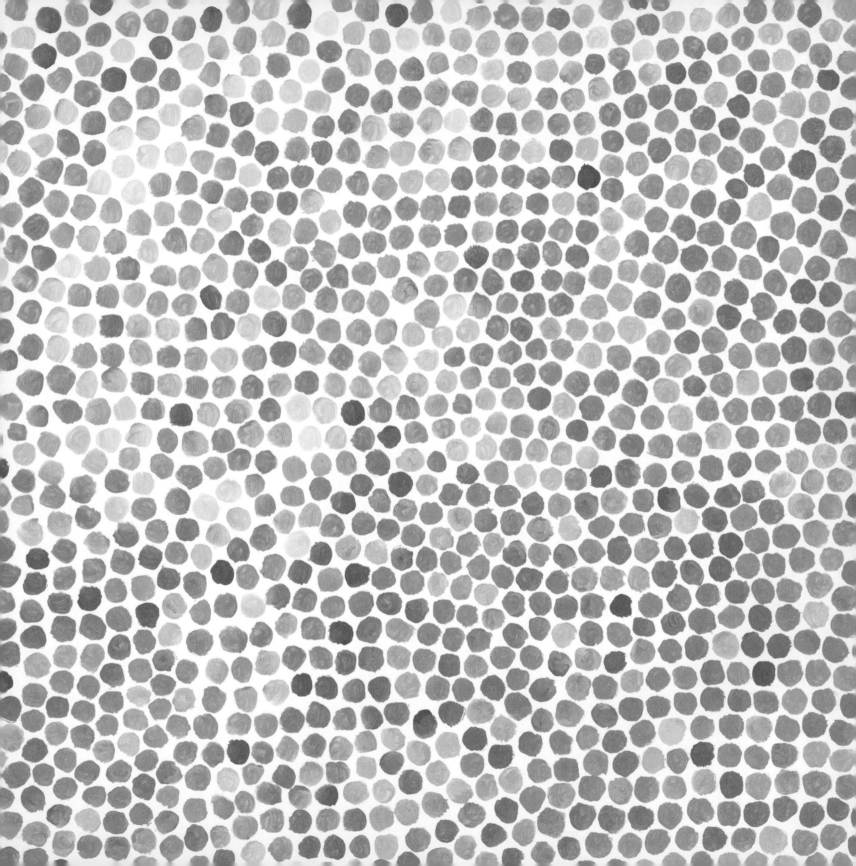